Elder Law:
Legal Planning for Seniors

Parker Press Inc.
Briarcliff Manor, NY 10510

ISBN: 978-1-941760-08-6

For the latest information and updates to this material, check out:
http://www.reallifelegal.com/updates

Elder Law:
Legal Planning for Seniors

**Maria B. Whealan, Esq.
and Susan G. Parker, Esq.**

Real Life Legal™

Helpful Guides for Everyday Legal Matters

Parker Press Inc.

Contents

Contents

What This Book's About

If you've experienced the decline of a dear friend with health problems, you worry about the loss of your own mental faculties, or your children are concerned about your future care, this book will help you understand how to get your affairs in order.

This book covers issues we face as we age. While it's a good idea to have a last will and testament no matter your age, this book does not focus on traditional estate planning. That's covered in more depth in *Estate Planning: A Road Map for Beginners*, by the same authors and also from Real Life Legal™. Here the focus is on additional concerns that take center stage as you get older. For example:

- Who will make health care or financial decisions for you if you can't?

- What will happen if you become ill and can't afford the care you need?

- How can you preserve assets for your family?

Just as young parents gravitate to baby books, seniors need to understand a variety of issues that come under the heading of "elder law."

What Does "Elder Law" Mean?

Elder law encompasses legal concerns that become important as we age. It covers legal documents that should be in place, as well as financial or health care issues you or your family may face if your health declines.

As the baby boomers cross into their sixties, their aging issues are important not only to them, but to their families and caregivers. The field of elder care continues to grow as the many issues that affect "seniors" do as well. In some circles, elder law covers everything that can impact an older person's life, such as workplace issues, housing, nursing home/caregiver arrangements and elder abuse. This book covers legal and healthcare planning and what happens if you don't.

The most important part of elder care is making decisions at a time when you can, for a future version of you. This includes signing documents to appoint others to act on your behalf, if you can't.

Getting a Lawyer to Help

We recommend you hire an attorney to help with planning and drafting documents you need for the future. A traditional attorney who handles "trusts," "estates" and taxes can get this job done capably for most people. If you are concerned about special needs or Medicaid planning, you may need a specialist.

All elder law or estate planning attorneys do not have the same experience or know the same things. Attorneys can call themselves "elder law attorneys" but standards are uneven. Make sure the attorney you hire has expertise in what you need.

Elder law can include:

- Medicaid eligibility, caregivers or nursing homes, and spousal refusal.

- Guardianship, conservatorship, special needs planning and Social Security disability.

- Tax planning for high-net-worth or Medicaid-asset protection.

Get a clear statement of fees and know what services will be covered before you sign a retainer.

Not all aspects of senior planning require an attorney. For example, you can apply for Medicare, Medicaid and Social Security benefits on your own. The federal government websites have a wealth of information to help you. Also, local offices in your town or county may help you navigate the process.

Legal Documents for Seniors

In addition to having a "Will" or a "living trust" to manage or distribute assets when you die, seniors need to designate an "agent" to make health and other decisions for them, if they no longer can.

In many respects, the legal directives you need in place when you get older are like insurance. Let's say you pay car insurance premiums for your whole life and never have an accident and never collect on a claim. The true benefit of the insurance is the knowledge that you won't face financial hardship if you have an accident. Insurance brings peace of mind and protects against risk.

It's the same with elder law planning. You create legally binding documents that authorize someone else to carry out your wishes concerning health care and financial management. If there comes a time when you cannot make these decisions on your own, the person you designate makes these decisions for you. If you remain healthy and of sound mind, these documents may never become operative.

One of the most important things you can do for yourself, your family or aging friends is to make sure someone can step in for them if they can no longer make decisions on their own. These decisions may include everything from who will pay the bills to who can help make health care decisions.

Three Legal Documents Seniors Must Have

Although all adults should have these documents "just in case," it's especially important for seniors to have them:

- **"Health Care Proxy"**: Appoints another to make health care decisions for you if you are unable to do so.

- **"Living Will"** or **"DNR"**: In some states a "living will" and a DNR are separate documents. A DNR technically describes when you will/will not be resuscitated, and the living will spells out your preferences regarding life-sustaining measures. Together they indicate your end of life decisions.

- **"Durable Power of Attorney"**: Appoints another as your **"agent"** or **"attorney-in-fact"** to manage your financial and other affairs. It remains in effect even upon the onset of a mental impairment such as dementia.

Wills and Trusts in Estate Planning

Unlike a Will, which speaks only from the moment of death onward, a trust speaks from the moment it is created. A trust is used to manage assets both during your life and after death. Both Wills and trusts have a place in estate planning for seniors.

A cornerstone of all estate planning, not just for seniors, is documenting how you want your assets to pass at your death. People commonly think that this is only done by writing a Will. But in reality, much of what we own and pass at death passes by operation of law.

Property held in trust, owned jointly in a bank account or by deed title, and property which passes from an IRA or life insurance policy via a "beneficiary designation form," does not pass to beneficiaries under your Will. These items pass to beneficiaries by operation of law.

The Importance of Having a Will

A Will is essential to pass property that you own in your name alone. Even if you have a "living trust" as part of your estate plan, you still need a Will to:

- Appoint a guardian for minor children and/or name a successor guardian for an adult child who is disabled.

- Appoint an executor to oversee the administration and distribution of your estate.

- Dispose of property that may not be held in your living trust.

In some states, your Will may also be the place you set forth burial wishes and anatomical gifts. States have different rules on how to make these wishes legally binding so you should check the state where you live to get it done right.

If you fail to write a Will, each state has "laws of intestacy" which provide a default setting to determine who will get your property. Contrary to common misconceptions, the state doesn't inherit your property; your next of kin do.

What Is a Trust?

"Trusts" are legal agreements that provide for the ownership, management and distribution of assets to named beneficiaries. A **"trustee"** is the person legally appointed as a fiduciary to manage the trust. Sometimes you can serve as a trustee of a trust you create.

Trusts can be created either as part of your Will (**"testamentary trusts"**) or during your lifetime (**"inter-vivos trusts"**).

- A testamentary trust only comes in to existence when you die, and it is funded with assets you leave to the trust under your Will.

- An inter-vivos trust is created during your lifetime, but can be funded either during your lifetime or at your death.

All types of trusts can be used to provide for: (1) continuity of management of assets and (2) a plan for distribution at death.

Trusts in Estate Planning

Trusts can be used for many purposes in estate planning. They are created to:

- Provide for both a new spouse and children from a prior marriage.

- Manage money for minor children under age eighteen or twenty-one.

- Make sure special needs beneficiaries can inherit property and still preserve any public assistance they receive.

- Give bequests to charities, universities or other institutions, while retaining some benefit from the assets.

- Own life insurance which may be needed to cover taxes or expenses of an estate.

- Get special tax benefits upon the transfer of:

    - Your home

    - Life insurance

    - Annuities

    - Collections

Living Trusts

A "living trust" is a common trust used in estate planning. It is called a "Will substitute" because it can be used to pass assets to your heirs when you die. Here's how it works:

- You create the trust while you are alive and transfer all of your assets into the trust.

- The trust is the legal owner, but you serve as trustee and can do what you wish with the property while you are alive.

- The trust agreement spells out what will happen with your assets after you die.

These types of trusts are particularly helpful for older people who want to consolidate their assets and simplify or avoid probate.

When a Will is offered for probate, what the Will says becomes a matter of public record. However, a trust does not get offered for probate. By leaving assets to heirs in a trust, privacy is maintained. Also, assets left in trust do not go through probate, and probate may be avoided depending on what else you own (apart from assets in a living trust) at death.

Revocable vs. Irrevocable Trusts

"Revocable trusts" are trusts you create and can change or revoke while you're alive. You can serve as a trustee and decide how you want to spend assets or give them away. The assets in the trust are included in your estate for tax purposes.

- These trusts generally do not have a separate tax I.D. (like your social security number) and income from the trusts is reported on your personal tax return.

- A living trust is one type of revocable trust.

"Irrevocable trusts" are created while you're alive but cannot be changed or revoked. To achieve certain tax or other benefits, you must put the assets "beyond your control." This means you cannot change who gets what and the trust agreement spells out how the trust will manage and distribute assets.

With an irrevocable trust:

- You cannot serve as a trustee and make decisions on how funds are distributed to you.

- The trust has its own tax I.D., and is a separate taxpayer.

- If you retain too much control, you may not achieve desired tax results.

The trustee is responsible for managing the trust's assets and making distributions to named beneficiaries. This can occur both during your life and at death. Often you are the trustee of your living trust or a revocable trust while you are alive.

Estate Tax Planning

Although the federal **"estate tax"** rate is 40% in 2014, most people don't pay estate taxes. Here's why:

- Every person has a $5.34 million (for 2014) estate tax exemption.

- If you are married and one spouse doesn't use up the exemption, the other spouse can use what's left, when he or she dies.

- You can make unlimited gifts and bequests to your spouse and not pay taxes or use your exemption. (This doesn't apply to non-citizen spouses.)

- Gifts to charities are generally exempt from tax.

The federal estate tax exemption is increased with cost of living adjustments. Almost half the states also impose some sort of estate or death tax. State estate tax planning can be important too, because state tax exemptions may not be as high as the federal tax exemption.

For high-net-worth individuals, tax planning is essential to reduce taxes.

This discussion is meant to introduce you to these topics in connection with planning for seniors. For more in-depth coverage of some topics mentioned here, check out additional Real Life Legal™ titles: *Estate Planning: A Road Map for Beginners* and *Planning for Your Special Needs Child.*

Signing Legal Documents

The laws of the state in which you live specify how Wills, trusts and advance directives must be signed to be legally binding. Often you must comply with certain formalities including having a signature witnessed or "notarized." "Due Execution" means you have properly complied with the formalities when the document is signed.

While all states provide similar rules, the details of properly executing a document are very important when it comes to estate planning. What is needed to have a valid document signing varies from state to state. For example, one state may require two witnesses for a Will to be valid, and another may require the witnesses appear with the Will signer in the same room at the same time, and that their signatures be notarized.

If a legal document is validly executed in one state, it will generally be honored in another. But if you move, it's a good idea to sign new documents in compliance with your new state's rules to avoid any potential problems.

Legal Capacity

You have to be of "sound mind" or have "legal" capacity to sign legal documents. If you don't understand and appreciate the consequences of your actions, the validity of the document can be called into question. Documents can also be challenged if they are not signed of your own free will.

Legal standards of capacity vary depending on the task at hand. For example, you need a high level of legal capacity to sign a business document. But to sign a Will, it may be enough to know who your relatives are and have a general idea of what you own.

REAL LIFE EXAMPLE

Betsy is eighty-five years old and in reasonably good shape. She has no children, but has named her younger brother, Henry, as the executor of her Will and has left her property in equal shares to Henry's four children.

When Henry dies, Betsy knows she has to change her Will to appoint a new executor. While Betsy is not quite sure what her assets are worth, she knows she has a lot of money and jewelry, and wants to now leave something extra to her niece Candace who visits her often.

Betsy meets with her lawyer to change her Will. The lawyer realizes that Betsy is not as mentally sharp as she was when he met her ten years earlier. Betsy is clear that she wants Candace to be her executor and to receive all of her jewelry, which was valued at $3 million, ten years earlier. Betsy also asks that Candace be paid executor commissions.

The lawyer is confident that Betsy has sufficient capacity to make the changes she requested. The lawyer writes an affidavit stating that he has met and interviewed Betsy and attests to the fact that she has the requisite capacity to change her Will, under the laws of her state. If any of Henry's other children later challenge the Will, claiming that Betsy was mentally failing, the lawyer's affidavit will provide strong evidence in favor of upholding the Will.

If the validity of a document you sign is ever called into question, a court would look at all of the facts and circumstances to determine if you had capacity and signed of your own free will. Things that may be considered include:

- Whether greedy caregivers were standing nearby as you signed a new Will leaving everything to them.

- Whether you were heavily medicated because of an illness at the time you signed your Will.

- Whether someone was pressuring you or "overreaching" you to name them in the Will, and you might have not been acting on your own.

If you have a lawyer oversee the process of signing legal documents, he or she can attest to your legal capacity if it is ever called into question. This is important if you anticipate there may be challenges to your plans.

Why Plan Now?

When planning for your older age, the law enables you to put documents in place *now* to ensure your intentions and plans are carried out later. What you decide while healthy and well, will be honored even if you no longer have your health or wits about you.

It is much easier and cost-effective to empower your loved ones or trusted advisors to make decisions if you no longer can, than to "hope" things will work out. If the proper documents are *not* in place, and you can't manage on your own, a court proceeding for a guardianship or conservatorship may be needed so someone can take charge of your affairs. The proceeding and the cost of the guardianship are expensive and it's much better to plan ahead.

Planning Puts You In the Driver's Seat

With a plan in place you can specify:

- What types of medical treatments you do or don't want.
- Who will help you with banking and financial matters.
- How your assets will pass at your death.
- How you'll pay for health care if you need it.

Health Care: Advance Directives

Health care directives are instructions to your doctors and health providers about what you want to happen if you can't make decisions on your own. These instructions can be important at any age, but seniors often have more health issues so it's important to have these documents in place.

Here's what health care directives do: Let's say you are in a car accident, or a complication has arisen after major surgery, and you are not lucid enough to make decisions.

- To get the required "okay" for any needed medical procedures, your medical team will look to your **"health care proxy."** This is a legal document that appoints someone to make health decisions for you if you can't.

- For doctors to take you off life support, they'd look at a legal document known as a **"living will"** or **"do not resuscitate"** order, to learn your wishes.

State laws spell out what these forms must say and how they must be signed.

It is never too early to plan but it can become too late.

What Is a Health Care Proxy?

A health care proxy (a.k.a. durable power of attorney for health care) appoints someone you trust to make decisions for you concerning health matters. These documents come into play if you are not lucid or lack capacity to make health decisions for yourself. The person you appoint is called an agent, a proxy, a surrogate or a representative.

As we age, it is more likely we will face some health issues that may require someone to make decisions for us. But it's a good idea for everyone to have a health care proxy in place—not just seniors.

If you can't speak for yourself, a health care proxy is your voice. It is usually quite clear to family and medical personnel when your health care agent must step in to make decisions. Your primary care or attending physician usually makes this medical determination.

The person you designate as your agent only acts when you cannot.

Choosing Your Health Care Agent, Proxy or Surrogate

The person you appoint as your agent must be eighteen or twenty-one, depending on the age of majority in your state. Select someone you truly trust because your agent may be called upon to make tough choices on your behalf. The person you choose:

- Should be aware of your decisions and comfortable with carrying them out.

- Be able to act in your best interest and handle potentially conflicting advice from close family members, if it occurs.

- Be available to act by phone or in person.

A health care proxy may be needed in an emergency so it's essential to be able to get in touch with your designated agent. For example, don't select your dearest cousin if he lives in the wilds of Alaska and has spotty phone service. Most health care proxy forms request a telephone number and address of the person appointed. You should also name an alternate in case your primary agent can't be reached.

Generally, the attending physician or an employee of the hospital where a patient is staying cannot act as the health care agent for that patient.

What a Health Care Directive Provides

Most state health care proxy forms ask for the following information:

- **Contact Info for Agent:** Name, address and phone number of an agent and alternate agent.

- **Special Instructions:** Your list of specific wishes regarding medical procedures, treatments and medications so that your agent knows what you want. For example, you may indicate you never want tube feeding or an amputation.

- **Specific Treatments:** In many states, there must be a direct statement that your agent knows your wishes about certain types of treatment such as nutrition and hydration, and can make decisions about these treatments. Often they may have "life and death" implications so the agent's authority must be clear.

- **HIPPA Statement:** Under the Health Insurance Portability and Accountability Act of 1996 (HIPAA), your agent must **"execute"** a HIPPA statement to be authorized to access your health records. Special permission is needed to access confidential patient records. In the real world, this is something that is rarely used.

- **Organ Donations/Anatomical Gifts:** If you choose to donate any or all or your organs after your death, you can do so on some state forms. Other states indicate anatomical gifts on a driver's license or other document.

- **Duration:** Health care directives typically remain in effect indefinitely unless you specify a cut-off date. For example, if you wanted to limit the directive, you may appoint a sibling to act "for my upcoming back surgery."

Once the requested information is filled out, your name, date and signature are required. Each state also has its own requirements about witnessing the form. Most states require that the form be signed in the presence of two adult witnesses. Your state may also require that the signatures be notarized.

Who Can Witness a Health Care Proxy?

Witnesses generally have to be disinterested parties. For example:

- The witnesses cannot be the agent or the **"principal."**

- Sometimes family members, spouses, heirs to the principal's estate, and health care workers are also disqualified as witnesses.

Some states mandate that a patient advocate must sign as a witness when you are a resident of a skilled nursing facility.

Getting a Health Care Directive Form

Many states provide forms online to be downloaded and completed. The "official" state forms include all the legalities required by the state law. If you cannot find your state's form online, try:

(1) State or local agencies, such as the office of the aging or the department of health.

(2) Local hospitals.

(3) Your doctor's office.

(4) Senior citizen advocacy groups.

An attorney hired to do your estate planning should also prepare a health care proxy and a Durable Power of Attorney, in addition to your Will.

For a listing of each state's legal requirements to complete a health care proxy form as well as some links to the actual forms, go to http://www.doyourproxy.org/states.htm, and check out the "Planning Ahead" suggestions at http://www.caringinfo.org.

Who Gets Copies of Health Care Directives?

Typically, your health care directive is kept with your important personal papers such as your Will, military discharge papers and the like. It is a good idea to give copies of the completed health care proxy to:

(1) The person you appoint as your agent.

(2) Your primary care physician.

(3) Close family members, including spouse and children.

(4) Close friends or neighbors, if you are single and without relatives nearby.

If you keep the document with other important papers in a safe place, be sure to tell your loved ones that you have a proxy form and where it is located. You may also want to carry a written notation (e.g., in your wallet or purse) of your agent's contact information.

Out-of-State Health Care Proxies

Health care proxies are signed in the state where you live. If you have a vacation home in another state and/or are traveling, typically the health care proxy should be honored elsewhere, as long as it was *properly signed* in your home state.

A Safe Deposit Box Is Not Necessarily a Safe Place

If you keep your health care proxy in a safe deposit box, others may not have access to it when they need it. Make sure important papers can be retrieved if you are not available to get them. Let those you trust know where this safe place is.

It's a good idea to get a separate health care proxy for each state that you spend a lot of time in. Hospitals can be skittish about relying on forms that don't look familiar to them.

For example, if you primarily reside in New York but go to Florida for the winter months, consider executing both the New York and Florida health care proxies. You may want to appoint different agents in each state based on physical proximity and availability of the agent.

Medical Providers Refusal to Follow Your Instructions

Some hospitals may refuse to honor health care decisions if they conflict with hospital policies. This can happen if the hospital has some religious affiliation that mandates a course of action. These types of cases are often heard on the news when they're based on religious or other moral beliefs.

Hospitals are obligated to inform you of these restrictive policies before you are admitted, and normally are required to transfer you to another institution that will honor your health care choices as stated in the proxy form.

Revoking a Health Care Proxy

Often the best way to revoke a proxy is to prepare a new one that specifically states you are revoking all prior ones. You can also revoke a proxy by notifying the agent. If there is a signed form "still out there," it will be difficult for others to know it has been revoked.

As a practical matter, this will only become a problem if there are family issues over who has authority to make these decisions. For example, one sibling may want to pursue one course of treatment, and another may not. For this reason, it is best to revoke a proxy in writing and execute a new one. Make sure to provide copies of the new form to your health care providers, close family or friends who may be called upon if the need arises.

If You Don't Have an Advance Directive or Health Proxy

Many states have adopted family consent laws, which allow family members or other individuals with a close relationship to you to make health care decisions for you if you can't and no advance health care directive exists. Practically speaking, the laws provide a useful safeguard to surrogate health care decision-making but are not effective in preventing long and costly court intervention in situations involving family disagreement, or if no appropriate surrogate or agent is available.

End-of-Life Care Decisions

Advance health directives come into play when you are lapsing into a place where medical treatment cannot make you better and death in short order seems likely.

A document known as a **"living will"** lets you specify what type of end-of-life care you want when the time comes. "Living will" is somewhat of a misnomer because it is often thought of as the document that authorizes doctors to "pull the plug."

Two other documents may also come into play:

- **"Do Not Resuscitate (DNR)"** is the order you need in place if you do not wish to receive CPR or electric shock in the event of cardiac arrest.

- **"Do Not Intubate (DNI)"** dictates that breathing tubes will not be inserted in the event of respiratory arrest.

DNIs are commonly ordered together with DNRs, and both are normally created when a patient has a serious health condition and is not expected to survive for a long period of time. Even if a DNR/DNI is in place, a patient will still receive medications, food, pain relief and other general medical care.

The patient or the health care agent can request a DNR, and the forms generally must meet specific state requirements, which can include being signed/approved by a physician.

Standards for the contents of a valid living will vary by state. The goal of the form is to make your intentions clear concerning end-of-life health care decisions. Some states combine the appointment of a health care agent and living will into a single health care form.

Differences Between Living Wills and Health Care Proxies

By definition, a living will covers end-of-life health decisions only. A health care proxy covers any type of treatment. A living will includes your intentions to withdraw or withhold life-prolonging measures. The health care proxy is broader because it covers all medical conditions and treatment, not just end-of-life measures.

A living will "speaks for itself," and its terms will be used to clarify or interpret your medical intentions. With a health care proxy, your agent "speaks for you" to express your medical intentions.

With a health care proxy, intentions can be written on the form itself but can also be more broadly decided by the agent based on your prior communications. If your agent can't be reached or located, your doctors can also refer to your living will for guidance.

It's best to sign both a living will and a health care proxy form to cover all bases.

REAL LIFE EXAMPLE

Bob goes into the hospital for hip replacement surgery. There are complications, and he is not lucid after surgery. Decisions have to be made about next steps, including a blood transfusion and the use of breathing tubes. Since Bob cannot communicate, his doctors will ask his health care agent, named in his health care proxy, to make the decisions for him.

If Bob's condition further deteriorates his doctors will look to his living will to learn his wishes regarding end-of-life care.

- If Bob's living will advises that Bob doesn't want to be kept alive by artificial means and the doctors determine he is "brain dead," they know what to do.

- If Bob doesn't have a living will, the decisions by doctors and family members will be more difficult. Doctors rarely "pull the plug" without a living will that provides permission.

Either way, in a worst-case scenario, there is the possibility that a guardian might be appointed if there are no advance directives and the medical decisions are controversial. A guardian may also be appointed if there is dissent within the family as to the course of treatment. In short, it is best to have a health care proxy and living will to avoid this unfortunate scenario!

Health Care Proxy vs. Power of Attorney

A health care directive authorizes another to make health care decisions for you. A power of attorney or POA gives authority for an agent to make other types of decisions for you.

Powers of Attorney (POAs)

A POA lets you appoint someone to act on your behalf with respect to financial, business, or other matters. What's known as a "durable" POA stays effective even if you become mentally incompetent.

With a POA, you (the "principal") grant specific authorities to another person (the "agent" or "attorney-in-fact") to act on your behalf in the matters you select. A POA includes a list of items that you can appoint your agent to handle for you—including things like banking or buying and selling property. All forms also have a check box for "all of the above."

The legal formalities for executing a POA are prescribed by state law. State laws tell you what you can and can't do with a POA.

It is important to consult with an attorney before you execute a power of attorney. There can be a lot at stake and often these forms are difficult to navigate if you haven't done one before.

General vs. Limited Power of Attorney

A **"general power of attorney"** gives broadly defined powers to the agent. These powers are set forth in the POA form, and typically include the ability to handle banking, financial, and other business matters for the "principal." Powers granted to the agent in a general POA include the right to:

- Buy and sell property.

- Handle banking and other financial transactions.

- Sign and file tax returns.

- Deal with all estate, insurance and retirement benefit matters.

- Obtain government assistance.

- Access safe deposit boxes.

- Hire and pay for attorneys, accountants and other professional advisors.

A **"limited power of attorney"** gives your agent the authority to act on your behalf only in specifically defined situations. For example, if you are unable to attend a house closing, you may execute a POA to appoint your spouse or attorney as your agent, solely to sign papers on your behalf at the closing. The agent would not have the power to do anything else except sign papers at the closing.

With a POA, you specify what authority you want your agent to have and under what conditions. For example, you may only want your agent to act if you suffer from a mental disability, but do not want the power of attorney to be operative if you are well and have your wits about you.

In some states, special language or execution formalities are needed if you want your agent to have the ability to make gifts with your money. This is often helpful for estate and tax planning and yet can be abused. Special forms known as **"riders"** may have to be signed by the principal and separately witnessed to make gifts under a POA.

Durable Power of Attorney

A power of attorney can be placed in effect for a certain period of time or until it is revoked. If the POA is *"durable,"* it means that the authority you give to another will last even if you become mentally impaired or disabled with diseases like dementia or Alzheimer's. A POA is a valuable planning tool and must be exercised very carefully.

A durable POA stays in effect if you are disabled, incapacitated, or otherwise unable to act. A regular POA is no longer valid if you are mentally incapacitated.

A "Springing" POA

A POA that only takes effect upon the happening of a specific event or circumstance is known as a **"springing"** POA. They "spring" into action only when an event occurs. A common example is when an agent's right to act on your behalf is triggered only if you become mentally disabled and can't act on your own.

Often people do not want others to have broad authority to act for them unless they cannot act on their own. In this situation, a springing durable power of attorney works best.

If you don't have a durable POA and end up with dementia or Alzheimer's, your family may be unable to manage your affairs. To avoid this result, if you appoint someone you trust to be your agent with a durable POA, you've got a better shot of having your wishes carried out.

Choosing an Agent for Your POA

With a POA, choose someone you trust who has some business sense. Unfortunately, even family members can be motivated by greed or financial desperation and can abuse their privileges as your appointed agent. For this reason, several states have recently revised their power of attorney forms to prevent this type of abuse and to make sure that principals have clear understandings of the powers of their agents.

At the least, you must appoint one agent. However, it is often a good idea to have two agents, with both signing off on any transaction. Although it is more complicated, your family dynamics may make it a good idea. You should also name an alternate agent who can act if the primary agent is not capable of serving.

REAL LIFE EXAMPLE

Dad is a widower in his late seventies with three grown children. Dad names Al, his oldest child, on the durable POA. Al has been in and out of jobs because of the economy. Dad's Will specifies that his children will share equally in his estate.

Al invites Dad to live with him in part so he can receive rent from Dad. After a trial period, Dad is glad for the home cooking and company and agrees it makes sense to stay with Al. Using the durable POA, Al sells Dad's house. Al remains unemployed and begins to use his father's funds as his own.

When Dad needs a care giver, the family learns that Al has sold Dad's house and spent most of Dad's money. Had two children been required to serve as Dad's agents, Al would not have had unrestricted use of Dad's funds. Both children would have been required to act together.

Common Questions About Powers of Attorney

Should a Lawyer Prepare a POA?

If at all possible, have an attorney prepare your POA. Here's why:

(1) A series of formalities must be followed in order for the document to be legally valid in each state. These formalities pertain to contents, signatures of the principal and/or agent, notarization and witness requirements. An attorney can make sure it's done right.

(2) The documents are complicated! While many states have their own statutory forms available online, they are not simple to complete. The fine print is very important in a POA and something that might look "simple" could have ramifications you don't really understand.

(3) Sometimes these forms have special parts that require additional formalities. For example, in some states you can appoint your agent, but the POA is not effective until the agent *accepts* the appointment. Other states require signatures to be notarized if an agent has a right to make "gifts" to himself. These details are important when it comes to a POA.

Who Should Get Copies of a POA?

You should give copies of your power of attorney to your agent and to the various institutions and agencies where you'd like your agent to handle your matters (e.g., banks, other brokerage/ financial institutions, or government agencies). When the time comes, you may discover that your bank, brokerage house or financial institution has its own POA form it wants you to complete. It is important to do so because you want your agent to be able to act if there comes a time when you need help.

You May Need Your Bank's Power of Attorney Form, Too

Although a validly executed POA should be honored, increasingly, banks and other financial institutions only honor a POA that is witnessed before its bank officers or executed on a bank-authorized form. These extra procedures are added to protect the bank from liability for honoring a POA that was obtained by fraud or no longer valid. CHECK THE RULES WHERE YOU BANK!

Can a POA Be Used to Make Health Care Decisions?

No! Only a health care proxy can be used to appoint someone to make health care decisions. A POA is used to manage financial and business affairs. You need both documents to cover all bases.

How Do I Revoke a POA?

The most common way to revoke a power of attorney is to execute a new one, which states it is revoking an old one.

You can also revoke a power of attorney form in writing by:

- Stating your intentions to revoke,

- Referencing the old power of attorney by date, and

- Giving the written notification to your agent and any institutions or agencies that have been relying on the existing power of attorney.

Often there is a space on the form that confirms the POA is valid as of a certain date, or you may be asked to provide such verification by your financial institution.

No POA, not even a durable one, is valid when the principal dies. In a minority of states, a divorce will also automatically revoke the power of attorney granted from one spouse to another.

Health Care Planning for Seniors

Seniors may receive benefits under Social Security, Medicare and/or Medicaid and private health care or long-term care policies. Getting the care and coverage you need as you age can be expensive and complicated.

Social Security, Medicare and Medicaid, Oh My!

Medicare is health insurance for individuals age sixty-five and over who are entitled to Social Security retirement benefits. Older Americans generally receive Social Security benefits accrued through their own work life, the working life of a spouse or because of disability.

When Medicare was enacted in 1965, the thinking was that working people would "pay in" to Medicare during their earning years, so that illness wouldn't ravage their savings in their later years. And yet now, almost fifty years after its enactment, Medicare is not the cure all many had hoped. Why? Because it doesn't cover the cost of long-term chronic care, which those facing diseases such as Parkinson's, Alzheimer's and dementia will need.

That's where Medicaid may come in. Medicaid provides benefits for home health care, nursing homes and other types of health expenses that are not covered by Medicare. It also provides insurance coverage for those with insufficient resources. Medicaid is funded by the federal government and the states.

Medicaid is administered on the state level, and each state has its own rules as to eligibility and benefits, within the federal mandates. Check your state's rules to learn the benefits available to you.

Paying for Health Care

For many seniors, paying for healthcare entails a patchwork of programs with Medicare as the core coverage. For medical care not covered by Medicare, you may look to your own private insurance, a Medigap insurance policy, long-term care insurance and/or Medicaid, for coverage.

The Affordable Care Act (a.k.a. ACA or Obamacare) creates new opportunities for seniors to obtain health care coverage. For those under age sixty-five who are not yet eligible for Medicare, there are new Health Insurance Marketplaces/Exchanges which offer sales of private insurance plans.

The marketplaces are either run by specific states or the federal government, and are intended to offer greater access to health care coverage to those who need it. All health plans must offer essential benefits in ten categories, such as emergency services, hospitalization and prescription drugs, and coverage cannot be denied for most pre-existing medical conditions.

While the ACA sounds great, important questions remain about the costs of health care plans under the law and, ultimately, whether people can afford to pay the premiums and deductibles on such policies. Stay tuned as the new program continues to roll out.

Complex Rules Apply to Medicare and Medicaid

Experts can help you decipher how government regulation and/or entitlements meet the real world. Plus, each state has its own way of administering these programs on a local level, within federal guidelines. Here our aim is to make you aware of the types of coverage and benefits you can expect, but you need to check your state for specifics.

The latest and greatest information on the following subjects is often found on federal or state websites. The federal government's Medicare website is excellent and walks you through the particulars of more than just Medicare. By merely entering your zip code, you can get the names of the Medigap and prescription drug coverage providers available in your area.

Make sure to check out the following websites for up-to-date information on these subjects:

- **Medicaid:** http://www.medicaid.gov

- **Veterans Benefits:** http://benefits.va.gov

- **Long Term Care Insurance:** http://www.ltcfeds.com

Medicare

Medicare is a federally sponsored program that provides primary health insurance for Americans age sixty-five and older, and for people younger than sixty-five who have certain disabilities and illnesses.

Medicare, which began in 1965, is the primary health benefit provider for U.S. citizens meeting any of the following eligibility requirements:

(1) Age sixty-five and older.

(2) Younger than sixty-five, but with certain disabilities and illnesses.

(3) Afflicted with Lou Gehrig's Disease (ALS) or kidney failure requiring either dialysis or a kidney transplant.

Enrolling in Medicare

Enrollment in Medicare is fairly simple for those nearing age sixty-five. There is a seven-month "initial enrollment period" which starts three months before the month of your sixty-fifth birthday and ends three months after. If you do not enroll during the initial enrollment period, additional enrollment periods are available thereafter, but may involve paying a higher monthly fee for Medicare as a penalty for late enrollment.

- If you're age sixty-five or older and you're receiving Social Security checks, you should be signed up automatically for original Medicare (Parts A and B) and should receive your Medicare card three months before your sixty-fifth birthday.

- If you're not receiving Social Security benefits, you must enroll in Medicare through the Social Security Administration (SSA) either online (http://www.ssa.gov) or in person at the local Social Security office.

For those not yet aged sixty-five, but entitled to benefits, enrollment works as follows:

- Enrollment in Medicare for people with Lou Gehrig's disease is automatic.

- For those with kidney failure, enrollment can be initiated after the diagnosis.

- With respect to other disabilities for which Social Security disability benefits are received, recipients are automatically enrolled in Medicare two years after qualifying for the Social Security disability.

There is a distinction between Social Security disability benefits, which are based on Social Security taxes paid on earnings, and Supplemental Security Income (SSI) benefits, which are paid to disabled and blind persons who have limited income and resources. With Social Security disability, the recipient is automatically eligible for Medicare two years after qualifying for the disability, while with SSI, the recipient is automatically eligible for Medicaid in most states.

What Is Covered by Medicare?

Medicare has four parts. Parts A and B are the most commonly known and referred to as **"traditional Medicare."**

- **Part A: HOSPITAL/In-patient Hospital Services:** Under Medicare, there is coverage for up to ninety days for each benefit period, with a sixty-day lifetime reserve.

- **Part B: MEDICAL/Doctors' Visits/Outpatient Services:** Once annual deductibles are met, Medicare generally pays 80% of the approved amounts for covered services, and the Part B enrollee pays 20%.

- **Part C: Private Supplemental Insurance/(Medicare Advantage):** Approved providers offer supplemental coverage for items or expenses that are not covered by traditional Medicare, for an additional monthly fee. You must be enrolled in Parts A and B to participate in Part C. Medicare Part C, was originally called Medicare + Choice.

- **Part D: Prescription Drug Coverage:** You must voluntarily opt in to Part D and pay a monthly premium to do so. Anyone enrolled in Parts A and B is eligible for Part D coverage.

Paying for Health Care Expenses Not Covered by Medicare

There are many health care expenses not covered by Medicare (e.g., copayments, deductibles and premiums under Parts A through D; hospital stays longer than one hundred days per "spell of illness" in a skilled nursing facility, etc.). As a result, people who need or expect to need more insurance usually supplement Medicare benefits. This can be done as follows:

- Purchase of additional Medigap policies to cover these additional out-of-pocket costs.

- Maintaining employer coverage (if possible on one's own or through a spouse's employer).

- Applying for Medicaid.

- Using benefits under a long-term care insurance policy.

- Using personal savings for medical expenses.

If you have additional health insurance coverage from an employer or elsewhere, Medicare is normally the secondary payer after the private health insurance pays.

Medigap Insurance

"Medigap" insurance is Medicare supplemental insurance sold by private insurance companies to help pay for medical costs that are not covered by traditional Medicare. Things not covered by traditional Medicare can include deductibles, copayments, coinsurance and other extensions of Medicare coverage.

Medigap insurance plans vary by the coverage they offer, the state you reside in and the insurance company that offers the coverage.

If you're interested in Medigap policies, check out http://www.medicare.gov. You can plug in your zip code and get a list of available providers in your area. This feature is also available to find prescription drug coverage.

In evaluating Medigap coverage, the most important items to look at are those that matter to you most. It may sound obvious, but as you go through the websites and examine what you need, it can be confusing. If you are on several expensive medications, you'll want the plan that provides the most coverage. If you require frequent physical therapy, you'll want to be sure that additional coverage is available.

REAL LIFE EXAMPLE

Chris Jones recently had open-heart surgery and was suffering from a back ailment that kicked in when he was turning sixty-five and enrolling in Medicare. He found it confusing to be taking up to fifteen different medications at one point and thought Medicare Part D would cover them all. Chris went on the medicare.gov website and learned that Medicare Part D covered only certain medications. As a result, not all of his prescription meds were covered. His out-of-pocket expenses were going to cost a fortune!

On the Medicare website, Chris was able to research which plans covered the cost of his prescription medications. The Medicare website gave him a list of insurance companies and an estimate of drug costs at the providers in his area. He was able to select a prescription drug plan that covered most of his medications at the most affordable rates.

While Medigap policies vary greatly in cost and coverage, nursing home care is only provided as a limited and short-term supplement to Medicare, and NOT on a long-term basis.

General information and assistance applicable to your state of residence about obtaining a Medigap policy can be found under the "Supplements & Other Insurance" tab of the http://www.medicare.gov website.

Medicare SELECT Policies vs. Medigap Policies

Medicare SELECT plans provide a limited network of doctors and hospitals participants must use to get full insurance benefits. If you go to a Medicare SELECT provider, you will get full coverage. Out-of-network coverage may be available in emergency cases.

- Medicare SELECT policies generally cost less than equivalent Medigap policies.

- Costs are kept down because the plan functions like a restrictive HMO, which doesn't cover out-of-network care.

- If you use an out-of-network provider, the original Medicare plan will pay its share of approved charges and you are responsible for the additional coinsurance fees.

Medicare SELECT is not available in all states, so you should check your state if you are interested.

How You Qualify for a Medigap Policy

You must be enrolled in Medicare Parts A and B to purchase a Medigap policy. If you are enrolled in Medicare Advantage (Part C), you should plan to stay with either Part C or switch to Medigap because Medigap will not pay out to Part C participants. Here are some other important rules:

- There is six-month initial open enrollment period for Medigap, which starts the first month that a person turns sixty-five and is enrolled in Medicare Part B.

- During this open enrollment period, you have a guaranteed right to purchase any Medigap policy available in your state irrespective of your health status.

- After the expiration of the open enrollment period, you may still apply for a Medigap policy, but the insurance company may consider your health status, and eligibility is not guaranteed.

Medicaid

Medicaid was designed to provide health care benefits for low-income and disabled people. It increasingly provides benefits to seniors who are unable to afford certain health coverage not provided by Medicare.

Medicaid covers a vast range of medical services, including long-term nursing home and/or home health-aide care. Medicaid is jointly funded by the state and federal government and administered separately by each state. The key to your Medicaid benefits depends on the eligibility requirements and benefits available under your state's program.

If elderly or disabled persons are receiving Medicare, they can also receive Medicaid (if they qualify) and Medicaid may pay for Medicare premiums, deductibles, co-payments and other services not covered by Medicare. If those receiving Medicaid have private insurance through an employer, spouse or parent, Medicaid will be billed as secondary insurance and will usually pay for deductibles, co-payments and other services not covered by insurance.

Unlike Medicare, Medicaid DOES cover long-term custodial care in a nursing facility and long-term home health care.

Medicaid Eligibility Requirements

To be eligible for Medicaid, you must be a resident of the state in which you apply for Medicaid benefits. Generally you are required to be a U.S. citizen. "Emergency Medicaid," however, is available to illegal immigrants and other non-citizens, including the homeless. Since Medicaid is a program for low-income people, assets and income must not exceed certain prescribed amounts (which vary by county and state) to be eligible.

- **Income Limits**. Generally, your monthly income must be below a specified dollar amount, or, in some states, you can "spend down" your monthly income by paying for expenses incurred to meet the income level.

  - There are different income requirements for applicants living in the community (at home with a caregiver) as opposed to applicants living in a nursing home.

  - Those receiving care at home in the community generally may retain more of their income than those who reside in a nursing home. However all income levels are extremely low.

- **Resource/Asset Limits.** Similarly an applicant's resources/assets must be below a certain level to be eligible to receive Medicaid. A person's assets/resources includes all of their property, with certain exceptions. For example, the following are considered "exempt" assets and not counted as an applicant's available resources:

  - One car.

  - Personal effects, clothing, household furniture and appliances.

  - A burial fund of approximately $1,500 and a prepaid funeral expense arrangement or burial plot.

  - A home up to a limited amount of equity determined by the state of residence.

To qualify for a homestead exemption, the Medicaid applicant must intend to return to the home to live. Otherwise, the applicant's spouse or minor, blind or disabled child must reside in the home. State equity caps can range from $500,000 to over $800,000 in some states.

Medicaid Planning

In cases where an applicant has resources but a prolonged illness or nursing home stay is anticipated, consider planning for Medicaid in advance. This may involve transferring assets to the applicant's family members or into a trust that will benefit them. Special rules apply to these transfers, including penalties and "look-back" periods.

Medicaid Look-Back Rule

Medicaid has a five-year time period during which it can "look back" to determine if assets should be counted for eligibility purposes. This comes into play for applicants who need nursing home care. Under the look-back rule, Medicaid will review financial records to see if you transferred assets to qualify.

Certain assets do not count as being "transferred" and are known as exempt transfers for purposes of the look-back rule. These include transfers made to:

- A spouse.

- A child under the age of twenty-one.

- A blind or disabled child, regardless of age.

- A child who has served as the applicant's caretaker and who lived in the home for the two-year period prior to the transfer.

- A sibling with an equity interest in the home.

If the applicant and a sibling jointly inherit a home that was owned by their parents, and lived in the home during the one-year period prior to the transfer, it will be exempt.

Transfers which are gifts will cause a period of ineligibility. If you transfer property and receive something in return, it is considered a transfer for value and not a gift. In short, if you give away assets, you may not be eligible for Medicaid benefits until the penalty period ends.

There is a five-year look-back period for assets you give away if you need nursing home care. It does not apply if you need what's known as "community care," which is care at home or in a daycare center.

If you seek Medicaid benefits for home health care as opposed to nursing home care, you'd be subject to what is known as "community care" eligibility requirements. This term refers to the person's ability to live as a member of the community in a private residence, not a nursing home.

Medicaid Payback Provisions

When a person who has received Medicaid dies, and has assets, special rules may require that those assets be used to repay benefits received. These rules depend on how the Medicaid benefits are offered in your state and each state has its own rules on payback.

Miriam was injured in a catastrophic car accident and received a large recovery that was placed in a self-settled trust, created in accordance with the laws of her state. The assets in this trust did not count towards determining her eligibility for Medicaid. Miriam qualified for Medicaid and only lived a few years after the accident.

At the time of Miriam's death, a million dollars remained in the trust. Medicaid had provided $600,000 of benefits to Miriam while she was alive. Under the laws of Miriam's state, Medicaid has the right to receive $600,000 pay back for the benefits it provided for her care. The $400,000 balance held in the trust, after Medicaid is repaid, will go to the beneficiaries named in the trust.

Medicaid payback provisions are beyond the scope of this book, but if you are interested in Medicaid planning, make sure to ask the attorney who does your planning whether any payback provisions in your state will apply.

Medicaid Planning with Trusts

Increasingly, people consider establishing Medicaid trusts so that their assets won't count as "resources" when they apply for Medicaid. These trusts can go by various names such as "asset protection trusts," or "income-only trusts." The primary goal is to preserve assets for your family, if there comes a time when you need to enter a nursing home. With careful planning, it is possible to receive Medicaid benefits and make sure your family savings are not wiped out.

Keep in mind that if you transfer assets to an irrevocable trust more than five years before applying for Medicaid, the amounts you transferred will not affect your eligibility. But if you need benefits during the look-back period, you may want to delay your Medicaid application. Why? Because the assets you transferred out will cause a period of ineligibility.

The value of the assets transferred, and the years remaining in the look-back period, get factored in to determine the period of ineligibility. Sometimes it makes sense to pay out of pocket and wait to apply for Medicaid until the five-year, look-back period comes to an end. Once the five-year look-back is over, the assets transferred do not create a period of ineligibility.

Medicaid planning to preserve family assets requires a lawyer expert in this type of planning. The rules are complex and property must be transferred out of your name, often at a time when you may not know if you'll need Medicaid.

For more information about the Medicaid rules and eligibility requirements by state, go to the official U.S. government site at http://www.medicaid.gov and select your individual state profile.

Long-Term Health Care Insurance

"Long-term Care (LTC)" insurance is a popular option for financing long-term care if you have money available to purchase the benefits. The premiums increase as you age, and often they do not end; it is expensive to get a fully paid policy (as you might with life insurance) in today's marketplace.

Policy provisions must be carefully read and understood because they vary from state to state. LTC insurance policies generally provide coverage for all levels of nursing home care, assisted living, home care (including in-home personal care), adult daycare, respite care, hospice care and Alzheimer's disease/dementia services and facilities. Generally these services are for health, personal or custodial care over long periods of time, and are either not covered or only partially covered by private health insurance, Medicare and Medicaid.

When Does LTC Coverage Start?

Coverage under LTC policies typically start when a person is not sick but needs assistance with one or more "activities of daily living (ADLs)," such as dressing, bathing, eating, personal hygiene, toileting, bathing, walking and physical mobility.

LTC Policy Features

There are six main factors in determining the cost of LTC insurance:

(1) **Person's age:** Premiums increase with age.

(2) **Person's health:** Premiums will be more expensive if health problems exist, and can result in the limitation of benefits available or inability to qualify for LTC insurance depending on the provider and plan.

(3) **Daily benefit amount:** Maximum dollar amount of coverage per day (e.g., $150, $200).

(4) **Benefit period:** Maximum length of time over which benefits will be paid, commonly ranging from two to six or seven years. Partnership plans should specify the required time period over which the premiums must be paid and at the end of which Medicaid eligibility kicks in.

(5) **Elimination period:** Time during which no benefits are paid (e.g., twenty to 120 days); the longer the elimination period, the lower the premium amount.

(6) **Inflation protection:** The increase in benefits to hedge against inflation, which often carries hefty annual premium increases.

LTC policies can have limits for pre-existing conditions. Typically, an insurance company may look back six months from the time of application for the existence of a pre-existing condition. The policy may not cover expenses related to such conditions, until six months have elapsed from the effective date of the policy.

LTC insurance also often excludes coverage for various circumstances such as mental and nervous disorders (other than Alzheimer's or other organic brain disease/dementia), self-inflicted injury or suicide attempts, alcoholism and drug addiction and treatments already covered by the government (e.g., under Medicare or Workers' Compensation).

LTC Insurance Planning in Tandem with Medicaid

LTC policies are often a good option in conjunction with Medicaid planning. Because of the five-year look-back rule, it is often tough to plan that far in advance. Each state regulates insurance and LTC insurance is no exception, but proper planning can make a big difference.

Jack purchases a long-term care policy that provides three years of coverage in a nursing home. His estate is worth about one to one-and-a-half million dollars including investment assets, a home and IRAs. After his wife died, Jack transferred his home and assets to an irrevocable trust for the benefit of his children. Three years later, he had a stroke and was unable to live alone. His children found a good nursing home for him.

Jack begins to receive benefits under the LTC policy that cover the nursing home bill. Two years after he moves into the nursing home, and five years after he transferred assets to the trust, Jack applies for Medicaid. The five-year look back period has ended and his assets and income are reduced sufficiently so that he no longer exceeds Medicaid eligibility limits.

The LTC insurance has given Jack flexibility to (1) delay his Medicaid application and (2) preserve assets for his family. Had Jack applied for Medicaid during the look-back period, Medicaid benefits would have been unavailable to the extent of assets transferred out during that period.

LTC Insurance Partnership Programs

"LTC Partnership Programs" are joint ventures between private insurers and state Medicaid programs through which individuals purchase LTC insurance for a specified time period, and, at the expiration of such time period, access to Medicaid is provided under special eligibility requirements.

- States have put in these programs because they reduce the state's Medicaid costs and some of the risk is shifted to this private insurance.

- Individuals benefit from these programs because they can maintain assets but still qualify for Medicaid, and avoid being subject to Medicaid estate recovery upon their death.

- The asset protection features of the partnership plans vary based on policy types and premiums, and, while Medicaid programs follow federal guidelines, eligibility requirements vary from state to state.

Currently, approximately forty states have federally approved partnership plans that must comply with uniform standards for federal income tax qualifications and various consumer and inflation protections. To track the states that are part of the LTC Partnership Program as well as those that have reciprocity agreements, see www.dehpg.net.

There are many variables involved in deciding whether or not to purchase LTC insurance. First, can you afford it? Second, is it worthwhile to have it now, or later on in life? Some type of cost-benefit analysis must take place to determine when to purchase the insurance. The younger you are, the lower the premiums, however the premiums continue for a longer period of time.

Failing to Plan: Guardianship and Conservators

States have a "default" setting if you fail to plan for your needs and somebody must be appointed to take the reins. Often a loved one or family friend will commence the state court proceeding to make sure someone is managing your affairs.

Many people put off planning because they are sure they will sidestep the failings and illnesses of old age and just die peacefully in their sleep without any of the ruckus. Despite what many see around them, magical thinking can be quite persuasive.

Whatever the reasons for failing to plan, the consequences mean difficult decisions will fall to your loved ones. If there is no family to step in, ultimately the state where you live can appoint a guardian/conservator to manage your affairs. This involves a court proceeding and can be expensive and difficult. It can be avoided entirely if elder care documents are in place.

In many respects, with age comes wisdom. But when it comes to planning for aging many think, "It won't happen to me." Don't let denial wipe out common sense.

Guardians and Conservators

When you're a kid, typically, your parents are your guardians, i.e., they have legal responsibility to take care of you. The concept is similar with court-appointed guardians. A **"guardian"** is a person formally appointed by a court to make decisions on behalf of another person. The person who needs minding is known as the **"ward"** or "incapacitated" person. Guardians can be appointed to have either full or limited authority over their wards.

A **"conservator"** refers to someone who makes decisions about a person's finances and assets/property. Usage of the terms *guardian* and *conservator* varies among states, and they may be used interchangeably. If this is an issue, you'll need to check out your state's rules.

When Is a Guardianship Needed or Required?

Generally, the appointment of a guardian may be necessary when:

- A person lacks capacity, either physical or mental, to manage his or her own affairs.

- There is potential for danger or serious harm to the person.

- There are no other voluntary provisions in place for another legally authorized person to assume responsibilities for the person.

Guardianships are considered to be "last resort" measures due to the costly, complex and lengthy legal proceedings required for put them in place. While a ward's well-being is protected, a guardianship often results in the loss of many of the ward's important legal rights, depending on the state law and specific circumstances.

The best protection against a court proceeding to appoint a guardian is proactive estate planning. With a valid durable power of attorney and health care proxy in place, you have made the best plan for a future version of you, who cannot manage on his or her own. Trusts can also be set up to achieve similar results.

Appointing a Guardian

Each state has its own rules for obtaining a guardianship, but there are common elements among them:

- A petition for guardianship must be filed in the appropriate court where the "alleged" incapacitated person resides.

- The court obtains sufficient evidence of the person's incapacity through medical evaluations and other sworn statements and may request independent evaluations or reports if needed.

- A hearing or trial may be held if the "alleged" incapacitated person contests the appointment of a guardian.

Often a relative or other person of interest who knows the "alleged" incapacitated person well and can act in that person's best interests, petitions for guardianship and is appointed as guardian. If there are no family members willing or able to serve, a health care administrator, lawyer or close friend may be appointed. The guardian must be an adult and must meet the specific legal requirements of each state.

Most states have adopted the **"Uniform Adult Guardianship and Protective Proceedings Jurisdiction Act (UAGPPJA),"** making it easier to enforce guardianships across state borders. Essentially, the Act provides a uniform set of rules for determining jurisdiction in a guardianship case and makes it easier to deal with issues that come up. For example, the Act:

- Establishes a "home state" for guardianship purposes irrespective of the ward's physical location.

- Allows for the transfer and registration of guardianship orders from one state to another.

- Avoids the need to file a new petition for guardianship when an incapacitated person moves out of state to be closer to a relative/caregiver, or relocates for other reasons.

In terms of legal cost savings, avoiding delays and permitting increased mobility for the wards, the benefits are increasing as this uniform act is adopted in more states.

Responsibilities of a Guardian

The guardian is responsible for all decisions pertaining to the ward as set forth in the court order granting the guardianship. The guardian is often required to consider the wishes and values of the incapacitated person as best as possible. As a court-appointed fiduciary, a guardian must act with a high degree of trust and in careful consideration of the ward's best interests.

Guardians are subject to ongoing court supervision to protect against abuses of power and mismanagement of the ward's assets. Typically a guardian must post a bond to ensure against potential financial losses or abuses. Additionally annual accountings and reports must be prepared and filed with the courts, and most courts must grant permission before major decisions are made, e.g., the purchase or sale of real estate, the decision to continue or terminate life support.

Benefits and Resources for Seniors

There are many benefits available to seniors under state, local and national programs, in the public and private sector. If you have a need, it's likely it can be met.

Information about benefits and programs for seniors is available online. For example, the website http://www.usa.gov has a "Senior Citizens' Resources" section under "Topics" that provides links for sub-topics like:

- Consumer protection.

- Education/jobs/volunteerism for seniors.

- Caregivers' resources.

- End-of-life issues.

- Housing.

- Healthcare.

- Legal information (age discrimination, Medicare, Social Security Act, other).

- Financial information (investments, tax counseling, estate planning, retirement planning).

- Grandparents' rights and assistance with raising grandchildren.

- Housing (reverse mortgages, in-home help, nursing home comparisons).

- Travel and recreation for seniors (senior discounts and other travel tips).

At the state and local level, there are numerous public, private, and other combined public-private and/or nonprofit organizations that provide invaluable services for seniors. Also check county and municipal resources as well, including:

- Libraries.

- Community centers.

- Senior citizen organizations and group homes.

- Colleges/universities with law schools and other areas of study impacting seniors.

Online Resources for Seniors

Organization	Website
AARP	http://www.aarp.org
Alzheimer's Foundation of America	http://www.alzfdn.org
American Association of Trust, Estate and Elder Law Attorneys (AATEELA)	http://www.aateela.org
American Bar Association: Section of Real Property, Trust and Estate Law	http://www.americanbar.org
Medicare Rights Center (MRC)	http://www.medicarerights.org
National Academy of Elder Law Attorneys (NAELA)	http://www.naela.org
National Elder Law Foundation (NELF)	http://www.nelf.org
National Center on Caregiving (a program of Family Caregiver Alliance)	http://www.caregiver.org
National Center on Elder Abuse (NCEA)	http://www.ncea.aoa.org
National Council on Aging (NCOA)	http://www.ncoa.org
National Senior Citizens Law Center	http://www.nsclc.org

Glossary

Agent/Attorney-in-fact: Person appointed in a "durable power of attorney" to act in another's place.

Conservator: This refers to someone who is appointed to make decisions about an incapacitated person's finances and assets/property.

Do Not Resuscitate (DNR): This is the order you need in place if you do not wish to receive CPR or electric shock in the event of cardiac arrest.

Do Not Intubate (DNI): This document dictates that breathing tubes will not be inserted in the event of respiratory arrest.

DNR (Do Not Resuscitate) and DNI (Do Not Intubate): Legal document that instructs medical personnel concerning a person's wishes concerning resuscitation and intubation in connection with end-of-life care.

Due Execution: Proper compliance with legal formalities (such as witnesses and notarization of a signature) when a document is signed.

Durable Power of Attorney: This legal document grants your agent's authority to act on your behalf, even if you become mentally impaired or disabled with diseases like dementia or Alzheimer's.

Elder Law: Legal concerns that become important to people as they age, roughly those age sixty plus; can refer to estate planning, Medicaid planning, long term health planning, asset protection, elder abuse, age discrimination and other areas of law that deal with aging.

Estate: All manner of assets or interests that a person owns and leaves behind at death.

Glossary

Estate Tax: A tax levied by the federal government and/or states, on the amount of assets that a person owns at death. States may also levy the same type of taxes referred to as "death taxes."

Execute: To sign a document with certain formalities, such as witnesses and notarized signatures, so that it is legally binding.

Fiduciary: One held to a high standard of care in dealing with property on behalf of another. Trustees and executors are examples of fiduciaries.

Grantor/Settlor/Creator/Principal/Trustor: This refers to the person who sets up a trust. Often the person who establishes a trust also funds it, but trusts may also receive gifts or contributions from other sources.

Guardian: A person appointed to care for a minor child or another person who cannot manage his or her own affairs.

Health Care Proxy: Document that appoints a person to act in one's place to make health care decisions. The person is referred to as a "health care proxy" or "agent."

Limited Power of Attorney: This document gives your agent the authority to act on your behalf only in specifically defined situations.

Living Trust: A type of trust created to own, manage and distribute assets while you are alive. This type of trust is often referred to as a "Will substitute" because it can also pass assets on death. Assets in these trusts avoid probate but are included in an estate for estate tax purposes.

Living Will: Legal document that states end-of-life care wishes. It is the "pull the plug" document and should not be confused with a Will or Living Trust.

Glossary

Long-term Care (LTC): Refers to insurance which pays benefits in the event nursing home or long-term home health care is needed.

Notarize: To legally verify a signature by requiring signers to produce identification that they are the person claimed. A notary may witness the signature or receive acknowledgement that the person producing identification has signed it and verifies the signature, in a manner prescribed by state law.

Probate: The legal proceeding that determines the validity of a Will and oversees the process of administering an estate in accordance with the directions in the Will.

Rider: A document that is used to make changes or add details to the basic legal form or document.

Special Needs Trust: Refers to a type of trust or planning needed for a person with a disability who may require public assistance and/or help in managing his/her financial affairs.

Traditional Medicare: This is a U.S. government program which provides medical coverage for older and disabled Americans; refers to Medicare Parts A (hospital) and B (medical).

Trust: A separate legal entity that is formed to own, manage and distribute assets in accordance with instructions set forth in a trust document. It is managed by a trustee who must accept his or her appointment.

Trustee: Person appointed in the trust document to manage property held in trust.

Will: Also known as a "last will and testament." It is the document that sets forth legally binding wishes regarding: how your assets will pass, appointment of a guardian, apportionment of taxes and appointment of an executor to manage the process.

About the Authors

Maria B. Whealan, Esq.

Maria B. Whealan practices in the areas of elder law, estate planning and administration and mediation. Ms. Whealan is a certified mediator who works in private practice and has served as Staff Attorney at the Women's Justice Center at Pace University Law School. Presently, Ms. Whealan also actively volunteers for Big Brothers/Big Sisters of Family Services of Westchester.

Ms. Whealan graduated from the University of Pennsylvania with a B.S. in economics from the Wharton School and a B.A., with honors, in Spanish. She received her J.D. from Rutgers Law School and is admitted to practice law in New York, New Jersey and the U.S. District Court for the District of New Jersey.

Susan G. Parker, Esq.

Susan G. Parker maintains a law practice in Westchester County, New York, which specializes in tax, estate and business planning. Ms. Parker graduated with a B.A. in history from the University of Pennsylvania and received her J.D. from St. John's University School of Law. She later earned a post-graduate law degree in taxation (LL.M.) from New York University School of Law.

Ms. Parker is licensed to practice law in New York and Florida, and the U.S. District Courts for the Eastern and Southern Districts of New York, as well as the U.S. Tax Court. Ms. Parker has written extensively on tax and legal subjects for legal publishers and financial firms for almost thirty years. Her first book, *Your Will and Estate Planning*, was published by Houghton Mifflin in 1989.

About Real Life Legal™

Parker Press Inc., the publisher of Real Life Legal™ creates plain language consumer information on legal, tax, business and financial subjects. Taking aim at info overload and legalese, Parker Press Inc. launched Real Life Legal™ in 2014. Real Life Legal™ provides practical advice, written by lawyers, to help people understand how the law works. Our goal is to provide solid, easy-to-understand information so *you* can decide whether it makes sense to hire a lawyer. Real Life Legal™ wants you to be prepared.

Available Titles

Bankruptcy Basics: Chapter 7 and Chapter 13
Marina Ricci, Esq.

Business Owners Startup Guide
Susan G. Parker, Esq. and Lynne Williams, Esq.

Elder Law: Legal Planning for Seniors
Susan G. Parker, Esq. and Maria B. Whealan, Esq.

Employee's Guide to Discrimination and Termination
Joanne Dekker, Esq.

Estate Planning: A Road Map for Beginners
Susan G. Parker, Esq. and Maria B. Whealan, Esq.

Filing a Homeowner's Claim: Natural Disaster or Not
Dawn Snyder, Esq.

A Lawyer's Guide to Home Renovations
John A. Goodman, Esq.

Available Titles (Continued)

Planning for Pets: Trusts, Leash Laws and More
Joanne Dekker, Esq.

Planning for Your Special Needs Child
Amy Newman, Esq.

Special Needs Education: Navigating for Your Child
Lynne Williams, Esq.

U.S. Veterans: Your Rights and Benefits
Maria B. Whealan, Esq.
with Paul M. Goodson, Esq.

What to Do When Someone Dies
Susan G. Parker, Esq.

You've Been Arrested: Now What?
Maryam Jahedi, Esq.

Notes

Notes

Notes

Notes

Notes

Notes

Notes

Notes

Notes

Notes

Notes

www.ingramcontent.com/pod-product-compliance
Lightning Source LLC
Chambersburg PA
CBHW060631210326
41520CB00010B/1560